SEARCH THE SCRIPTURES

an approach to chapter analysis Bible Study

NAVPRESS

A MINISTRY OF THE NAVIGATORS
P.O. Box 1659, Colorado Springs, Colorado 80901

Second Printing, 1975
ISBN 0-89109-070-3

The Navigators is an international,
interdenominational Christian organization.
Jesus Christ gave His followers
a Great Commission in Matthew 28:19,
"Go therefore and make disciples
of all nations . . . ." The primary aim
of The Navigators is to help fulfill
Christ's Great Commission by making
disciples and developing disciplemakers
in every nation.

Contents

Introduction

The Bible is a closed book to many people who find it difficult to understand.

For many other people the Bible is an open, exciting book. Its truths, like gems, enrich their lives.

One key to "opening the Bible" is systematic Bible study. A thorough, planned approach to Bible study on a regular basis will enable you to discover many enriching truths that are unavailable to the casual observer.

There are three units in this booklet:

- *The Basics of Bible Study* will give you general background information which applies to all methods of Bible study.

- *The Navigators Search the Scriptures Method* will introduce you to one approach to chapter analysis Bible study.

- *Improving Your Bible Study Skills* presents additional information and methods for continual development.

Unit One:
The Basics of
Bible Study

Know Your Goal

God wants you to be like His Son, Jesus Christ. "For those whom He foreknew He also predestined to be conformed to the image of His Son... " (Romans 8:29). The transformation of your life into the likeness of Christ will enable you to join in fulfilling creation's eternal purpose — to glorify the Creator.

Conformity to Christ is a life-long process which is only completed when you pass into God's presence. Paul described the process, "and all of us, with faces uncovered, because we continue to reflect like mirrors the splendor of the Lord, are being transformed into likeness to Him, from one degree of splendor to another, since it comes from the Lord who is the Spirit" (II Corinthians 3:18 Williams).

Bible study is a vital part of this process. If you will faithfully study God's Word, pray for understanding and diligently apply it to your experience, your life will change and increasingly glorify God.

Many spiritual truths have thought-provoking parallels in the physical world. Take, for example, a thirsty person coming to a well to drink. Before he can quench his thirst he must let down the bucket, draw the water and take a drink.

Similarly, God's Word is able to satisfy the spiritually dry and thirsty person. First, however, he must study to draw out the truths from the Bible and then personally apply them to his own life.

The drawing of the water is analogous to the academic study of God's Word. Good study methods and habits are essential to the proper understanding and application of God's Word. "Do your best to present yourself to God as one approved, a workman who has no need to be ashamed, rightly handling the word of truth" (II Timothy 2:15).

Drinking the water is analogous to believing and applying God's Word. "But he who looks into the perfect law, the law of

liberty, and perseveres, being no hearer that forgets but a doer that acts, he shall be blessed in his doing" (James 1:25).

Getting Ready

Good Bible study methods alone cannot guarantee a changed life. The Bible can only be fully understood with the aid of the Holy Spirit. Apart from a growing personal relationship with God, the academic study of the Word will produce little change. Some important steps of personal preparation are...

A Cleansed Life.

Refusing to deal with sin in your life breaks fellowship with God. The secret of restored fellowship and the cleansed life is very simple. "If we confess our sins, He is faithful and just, and will forgive our sins and cleanse us from all unrighteousness" (I John 1:9). Before beginning your Bible study, stop to confess to God any known sins.

Prayer for Illumination.

Follow the example of the psalmist as he prayed, "Blessed be Thou, O Lord; teach me Thy statutes!... Open my eyes, that I may behold wondrous things out of Thy law... Make me understand the way of Thy precepts, and I will meditate on Thy wondrous works... Confirm to Thy servant Thy promise, which is for those who fear Thee" (Psalm 119:12, 18, 27, 38).

Dependence upon the Holy Spirit.

"Now we have received not the spirit of the world, but the Spirit which is from God, that we might understand the gifts bestowed on us by God" (I Corinthians 2:12). God has given Christians the Holy Spirit to teach the truth from the Bible. Rely on His instruction. "Trust in the Lord with all your heart, and do not rely on your own insight" (Proverbs 3:5).

Willingness to Obey.

Jesus pointed out that a prerequisite to knowing the truth is the willingness to obey the truth. "... if any man's will is to do His will, he shall know whether the teaching is from God or whether I am speaking on my own authority" (John 7:17). A man who is willing to obey will receive God's instruction.

Basic Beliefs

The conclusions that a person draws from his study of Scripture reflect his basic beliefs about the Bible. There are four foundational beliefs which lead to proper understanding of Scripture.

The Bible is the Literal Word of God.

"All Scripture is inspired by God ... " (II Timothy 3:16). This statement is the foundation for this booklet. Because the Bible is God's communication to men, it deserves careful study and investigation.

The Bible is literal in the sense that its accounts are records of actual happenings, not myths or legends. There are, however, figurative statements, allegories and symbols used in the Bible.

The Bible is God's Means
to Communicate Truth to His People.

Man alone cannot discover God's plans — God must reveal them. God's truth is not revealed in the silent contemplation of your own life and experience but through the Holy Spirit's illumination of Scripture. "... 'If you continue in my word, you are truly my disciples, and you will know the truth, and the truth will make you free' " (John 8:31,32).

The Bible is Authoritative.

The Bible has authority because God is the author and has absolute authority over men. Every area of a man's life is subject to the Word. "... 'Man shall not live by bread alone, but by every word that proceeds from the mouth of God' " (Matthew 4:4).

For Every Passage There is
One Intended Meaning and Many Applications.

The Bible is God's Word, but God used men to pen what He intended. The first objective in Bible study is to understand what the writer was thinking. The intended meaning is found by examining the context of the passage, the customs of the day and the meanings of the words. Only when you have an understanding of the meaning can you correctly apply God's truth.

Keeping on Track

In order to handle the Word of God properly, it is necessary to follow certain guidelines. Observing these guidelines does not always guarantee correct conclusions, but disregarding them frequently leads to error.

Here are some basic rules that are frequently neglected. While they are not difficult to understand, care must be taken to not inadvertently break them.

Interpret Your Experience by the Scriptures; Do Not Interpret the Scriptures by Your Experience.

When people interpret the Scriptures by their experience, their experience becomes the standard of authority. In reality the Bible is the standard. Your life is under its authority.

Whenever a Christian universally applies a method to others that has worked for him, he is in danger of transgressing this principle even though the method itself may be a good application of a biblical commandment. A good example of this is the man who had difficulty with deficit spending and abolished all forms of buying on credit. He was so successful in overcoming his problem that he insisted that anyone owning a credit card or buying on time violates the scriptural injunction, "Owe no one anything..." (Romans 13:8). At this point the individual has interpreted the Scripture in light of his experience, making his experience normative rather than the biblical principle.

Do Not be Dogmatic Where the Scriptures are Not.

There are many areas in which the Bible is not conclusive. Take care not to say more than the Bible does. In many issues such as personal appearance, style of dress, standard of living or church government, a person needs to arrive at his own conclusions even though the Scriptures are not conclusive. In these situations a stand may be taken, but do not be critical of those who accept a differing view. Love should prevail.

Study a Passage in Context.

To determine the full meaning of a passage, its setting must be carefully considered. A passage should be studied in its *historical, cultural* and *textual* context. (The textual context includes the preceding and succeeding passages.) When Paul said, "The women should keep silence in the churches," he was not prohibiting women from singing in church. This statement was made in the context of a passage about tongues and prophesying.

Be Careful in Determining Whether a Passage is Figurative Rather than Literal.

You should consider a passage figurative when the Bible says the passage is figurative. Many times the Bible indicates in the text that a particular passage is to be taken figuratively. Occasionally the events, situations or places may be literal as well as figurative. Galatians 4 states that Mt. Sinai is a symbol of bondage and Jerusalem is a symbol of grace. These are literal geographic locations which are also symbols of spiritual truth.

You should also consider a passage figurative when the statement is out of character with the thing described. For example, a statement may be considered figurative whenever an

MT. 19:24

inanimate object is used to describe a person or animate being. In the Gospel of John, Jesus is referred to as "the Door," "Bread," "Water," etc. These words are all used in a figurative sense.

In Philippians 3:2, Paul warned "Look out for the dogs." He is describing a group of heretics teaching the necessity of circumcision for salvation. Thus, "dogs" is to be taken figuratively. Jesus says in Luke 13:32, "Go and tell that fox" referring to Herod. Thus, it can be assumed to be figurative.

Generally, it is easy to determine from the passage itself if the statement is figurative and to whom it refers. A study of parallel passages on the statement, however, often supports the interpretation. For example, the word "lamb" refers to Christ both in Isaiah 53:7 and John 1:36.

There are times when the same word is used figuratively but has different meanings in different places in the Bible. For example, "lion" in I Peter 5:8 refers to Satan, but "lion" in Revelation 5:5 refers to Jesus Christ. Generally the correct meaning of the figure can be determined by the context.

A word does not have a figurative and literal meaning at the same time. When a word in a sentence is given a figurative meaning, it supercedes the literal meaning. If the literal interpretation fits, it should be used unless the context makes it impossible.

Do Not Rationalize the Scriptures.

Do not attempt to interpret biblical statements by current philosophies and contemporary scientific theories. These thoughts often change with the passage of time. The Bible, however, is eternal and never changes. For many years secular historians discredited the Bible's accuracy because there was no archeological evidence for the existence of the Hittite nation referred to in Scripture. Then in 1907 archeologists discovered tablets in Turkey which confirmed the existence and location of the Hitittes.

It is never necessary to apologize for the biblical statements that science cannot confirm or to reinterpret Scripture in the face of current scientific evidence. Because the Bible is God's Word and literally true, every miracle and every statement must also be considered true.

Do Not Spiritualize the Scriptures.

In an attempt to find so called "spiritual truths" in every verse, many people "read into" a passage a true conclusion that is determined by an invalid process. When a man uses a wrong method to arrive at a true conclusion, he opens himself to being deceived by that same method on other occasions.

For example, Acts 28 relates how Paul was miraculously healed after being bitten by a poisonous viper. Someone spiritualizing this account might say "the serpent, who is the devil, always attacks righteous men, but is always defeated."

This conclusion may be true, however, Acts 28 does not teach this conclusion. This is erroneous handling of God's Word.

Practicing the Essentials

In order to achieve the final goal of a changed life it is important to know how to make good personal applications from Scripture. The essential steps to making a good application are observation, interpretation, correlation and application.

Observation

Observation is the act of seeing; taking notice of things as they really are; the art of awareness. Observation depends upon two root attitudes — an open mind and a willing spirit.

Too often people approach Bible study with preconceived notions. Their attitude is "Don't confuse me with the facts; my mind is made up!" An open mind is necessary for effective study.

A willing spirit is necessary because whenever you guard an area of your life, you hinder understanding. The man who is

observation

unwilling to be changed in his marriage will not even see his needs as a husband. The woman who refuses to admit to vanity in her life will probably not see it condemned in the Scriptures.

Accurate observations are the result of reading with diligence, purposefulness, thoughtfulness and inquiry. Reading is not a lazy man's art. Reading until the Word jogs the mind and heart requires quality time. As you study, read for the message, not the mileage.

"Observation demands concentration! The purpose of observation is to saturate yourself thoroughly with the content of a passage. Like a sponge you should absorb everything that is before you."
                                                                    Oletta Wald*

It will help to record what you observe. As you write down your thoughts they become clearer. Get a study Bible which you can use for underlining important words, writing in the margins and drawing arrows to connect associated terms.

Be sure to define important words and phrases. Without knowing the meanings of words, it is impossible to communicate. One of the best reference books for Bible study is a dictionary.

Some questions to ask in making observations:

Who – Who are the people involved?

What – What happened? What ideas are expressed? What resulted?

Where – Where does this take place? What is the setting?

When – When did it take place? What was the historical period?

Why – What is the purpose? What is the stated reason?

How – How are things accomplished? How well? How quickly? By what method?

Interpretation

Interpretation is the step of determining the author's meaning. Interpretation seeks to clarify the meaning of a passage and help you understand why the Holy Spirit included this portion in

* From *The Joy of Discovery* by Oletta Wald,
Copyright 1956 by Bible Banner Press, Minneapolis, Minnesota. Used by permission.

interpretation

Scripture. Interpretation answers the question, "What does it mean?"

The Bible is the literal Word of God and means what it says. However, there is often more than one definition of a word. Correct interpretation depends on determining the definition the writer had in mind.

Correlation

Correlation is the process of relating the passage under consideration to the rest of the chapter, the whole book and other portions of Scripture. This prevents meanings from being forced on a passage which are not intended by the writer. Since the Bible is truth and all truth is unified, all interpretations must be consistent and coherent with the rest of the Bible.

One word of warning. The human mind cannot understand all that God has revealed. When established teachings in the Scriptures appear contradictory, both truths should be accepted in the confident belief that they will resolve themselves into a higher unity. How Jesus could be both human and divine is difficult to understand. It must, however, be accepted and believed.

correlation

It is particularly important to look for the paragraph divisions in a passage and consider each verse in the light of its relationship to the paragraph as a whole. Sometimes a paragraph may overlap a chapter division. In this case it is necessary to disregard the chaper division in order to fully understand the author's intent.

Application

Application is putting God's Word into practice — recognizing the voice of the Lord, and responding accordingly. "When I think of Thy ways, I turn my feet to Thy testimonies; I hasten and do not delay to keep Thy commandments" (Psalm 119:59, 60).

The benefit of Bible study is not derived from the method, the technique, or diligent efforts to decipher the text. The benefit is in obeying the voice of the Lord — receiving what He says and putting it into practice. Application doesn't happen by osmosis nor by chance — application is by intent!

Application starts with the willing acceptance of truth. A right response to Scripture is characterized by trust, obedience, praise and thanksgiving. The application may include remembering an impressive truth, changing a wrong attitude or taking a positive action.

Respond to God, not a rule book! Responses are to be motivated by love. The goal is to glorify God by pleasing Him in every area of life. An unwillingness to apply the Scriptures personally may develop mere intellectual knowledge and spiritual insensitivity to the Lord and to people.

The following list of seven directive questions may help you apply the Word to your life. *

1. Is there an example for me to follow?

2. Is there a sin for me to avoid?

3. Is there a command for me to obey?

4. Is there a promise for me to claim?

5. What does this particular passage teach me about God, or about Jesus Christ?

6. Is there a difficulty for me to explore?

7. Is there something in this passage that I should pray about today?

* From *How to Give Away your Faith* by Paul Little
© 1962 by Inter-Varsity Christian Fellowship.
Used by permission of InterVarsity Press.

application

An Example of Essential Elements

Consider how these elements of Bible study might be utilized in studying I Thessalonians 1:5, "for our gospel came to you not only in word, but also in power and in the Holy Spirit and with full conviction. You know what kind of men we proved to be among you for your sake."

Observation: 1) The Gospel Paul preached to the Thessalonians had a greater effect than mere words (verse 5).

2) The Thessalonians were aware of the kind of life Paul lived (verse 5).

Interpretation: Paul's exemplary life was one reason the Gospel had power.

Correlation: I Thessalonians 2:10 states what the Thessalonians knew about Paul — his holiness, justice and blamelessness.

Application: I need to concentrate on living a life of holiness as I tell others of Jesus. In particular I need to correct my critical attitude toward those who are not immediately receptive to what I say.

Summary:
Unit One

Know Your Goal

The objective of Bible study is to glorify God as you change into a more Christ-like person.

Getting Ready

1. A cleansed life
2. Prayer for illumination
3. Dependence upon the Holy Spirit
4. Willingness to obey

Basic Beliefs

1. The Bible is the literal Word of God.
2. The Bible is God's means to communicate truth to His people.
3. The Bible is authoritative.
4. For every passage there is one intended meaning and many applications.

Keeping On Track

1. Interpret your experience by the Scriptures; do not interpret the Scriptures by your experience.
2. Do not be dogmatic where the Scriptures are not.
3. Study a passage in its context.
4. Be careful in determining whether a passage is figurative rather than literal.
5. Do not rationalize the Scriptures.
6. Do not "spiritualize" the Scriptures.

Practicing The Essentials

1. Observation
2. Interpretation
3. Correlation
4. Application

Unit Two:
The Navigators
Search The Scriptures
Method

The Approach

In using the *Search the Scriptures (STS)* approach to Bible study, you will move from the *whole* to the *particulars* to a *conclusion.* The whole must be grasped before the particulars become meaningful. Understanding the meanings of the particulars leads to proper conclusions.

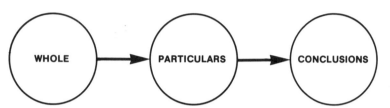

To illustrate, consider the possibility of studying one battle in World War I. Before any meaningful study can occur, it is necessary to know who fought in the war, why the war was fought, who won and what was resolved by the war. Next, it is helpful to know about the major campaigns in the war and how they contributed to the balance of power and the final outcome. At this point, a specific battle can be studied meaningfully.

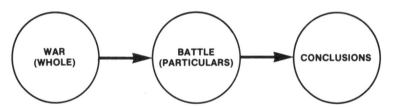

After a thorough study of the battle, you are able to draw some conclusions concerning the significance of this battle and how it was won. On the basis of these conclusions, you may discover modern parallels.

The approach to Bible study is analogous. The *STS* Bible study is a chapter analysis type of Bible study. It is usually used in studying a book by spending one or two weeks on each chapter of the book.

There are three steps to studying a book: the book survey (whole), chapter analysis (particulars) and book summary (conclusions).

There are also three steps to chapter analysis: the passage description (whole), the verse-by-verse meditation (particulars), and the theme and conclusion (conclusions).

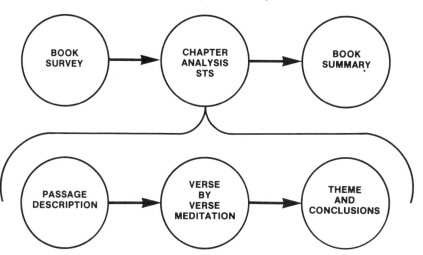

Since application may come from any step of the Bible study, it is not listed in the sequence above. The above order represents the steps used to discern truth from God's Word. Application involves putting this truth into practice.

How To Do
A Book Survey

A book survey gives you a sweeping overview of the entire book. This overview will help you understand and relate the particulars you discover later. A completed book survey form for I Thessalonians can be found on pages 37 and 38. Parts of this form will be used throughout this chapter to illustrate how to do a book survey. There are five sections to the form, "Principal Personalities," "Historical Setting," "Purpose," "Theme" and "Overview." Each section answers certain questions.

Principal Personalities

Who is the author? The recipient? Other major personalities? How do they relate to one another? How well do they know and understand one another? Here is an example from I Thessalonians of how this section might be handled:

STS Book Survey

Book _I Thess._ Date _7-10-74_

Principal Personalities: _Paul, the author; Timothy and Silas (Silvanus), co-workers with Paul while he ministered to the Thessalonians_

Historical Setting

When was it written? What is the historical setting in which it was written? What is the historical background of the recipient? Look again at an example from I Thessalonians:

Historical Setting: _Paul, Silas and Timothy went about 100 miles southwest of Philippi to Thessalonica (Acts 17) They spent about three weeks there and a growing church was begun. Paul probably wrote this letter after his visit while in Athens (A.D. 52) this is the earliest of Paul's epistles._

Purpose

Why was it written? If there is a problem to correct, what is it? What is the writer trying to accomplish?

Purpose: _To help overcome problems with Paul's character and ministry, to instruct on the doctrine of the return of Christ and to encourage them while they were being persecuted_

Theme

What is the major emphasis of the book? What are the recurring ideas?

Themes: _The Second Coming of Christ_
Paul's Personal Ministry
Purity of Life

Overview

Summarize the book in an outline, chart or diagram form. One possibility is for you to use the theme and outline as it is given in a reference book for a starting point as was done in the illustration at the end of the chapter. As you complete your study of the book you may wish to restate the theme and outline. For an example see the outline on page 38.

While these are not the only questions you can ask, they are the most important. Other questions might include:

1. What is the style of writing? For example, does the author use illustrations, present logical arguments, etc.

2. What are the key words?

3. What is the life-style of the recipients? What is their culture like? What are their customs, habits, etc.?

4. How does the geography and topography of the sites mentioned help you understand the book?

There are many possibilities. Some of these questions become more important in studying particular books. The more you study, the more you will be able to discern which questions are important to ask.

There are a variety of sources which can supply the information required for the survey. Most of the facts necessary to answer the basic survey questions are well documented. The theme and outline of the book may vary from one reference book to another.

Much of the background material necessary for doing a book survey can be found in the following reference materials:

1. *International Standard Bible Encyclopedia*

2. *Unger's Bible Handbook*

3. *Unger's Bible Dictionary*

4. *The New Bible Dictionary*

The following books give excellent outlines and themes of the books of the Bible.

1. *The Bible Book by Book,* G. Coleman Luck

2. *Through the Bible,* J. Sidlow Baxter

3. *What the Bible is All About,* Henrietta Mears

Don't be afraid to use reference material. These books usually reflect years of study done by men of God. On the other hand, do not rely on them completely. They are not infallible.

don't avoid
reference material

How To Use The STS Blank

When preparing the *Search the Scriptures* chapter analysis Bible study, you will begin with a passage description, then do a verse-by-verse meditation followed by your theme and conclusion. All these parts will contribute to your application.

The *STS* Bible study incorporates the four Bible study essentials of observation, interpretation, correlation and application. In the passage description you will make *observations* on the passage as a whole. In the verse-by-verse meditation you will make *observations* on each verse, ask questions to help you *interpret* the verse and use cross-references to *correlate* the verse with the rest of the Bible. You will draw these thoughts together and record them in the theme and conclusion section. Finally, you will record your *application* in the application section.

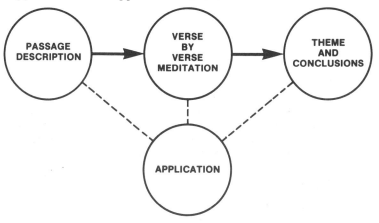

How To Do A Passage Description

Read through the passage several times and briefly describe the overall contents. While you may want to supplement your reading from one to the modern Bible translations or paraphrases, be sure to use one of the following for your basic study: King James, American Standard, New American Standard or the Revised Standard Version.

Do not attempt to analyze or interpret when writing your passage description. Carefully observe what is being said; not why. After reading your passage description, another person familiar with the passage should be able to identify it. While there are many ways to describe a passage, the basic content of the passage should be uniform.

AND FURTHER IT IS APPARENT THAT THE SUSPECT SUFFERED FROM A SEVERELY RESTRICTED MOTIVE FORCE RESULTING IN A PRONOUNCED AFFINITY FOR ABBERANT MANIFESTATIONS OF BOTH NEUROTIC AND MORAL ANXIETY WHICH COMMONLY STEM FROM AN EARLY FUSION OF INSTINCTS INTO A PHONORIOUS CONGLOMERATION OF SELF-IMPOSED ANTI-CATHEXES!

... WHICH LEADS TO THE ULTIMATE CONCLUSION THAT THE MORBID PATHOLOGICAL DISPOSITION EXHIBITED BY THE SUSPECT INDICATES A VAST AND PERNICIOUS, PRE-CONSCIOUS COGNITIVE STATE WHICH HAS INDUCED PROFOUND, INGRAVESCENT MELANCHOLIA CULMINATING IN A DELUSIONAL ABROGATION OF INTEREST IN THE RIGHTS AND PERSONAL POSSESSIONS OF OTHERS!

describe, don't analyze

Remember to use the principles of observation which were discussed in Unit I. Do not overlook the obvious in your description.

One method of describing a passage is to rewrite the passage without the modifying phrases and clauses. This basically leaves the subject, verb and objects. This approach is especially effective when the passage contains many modifiers. Using this method on I Thessalonians 1, your description might look like this:

> Grace to you (vs. 1)
> We give thanks to God for you (vs. 2-4)
> Our gospel came to you (vs. 5)
> You became imitators of us (vs. 6)
> You became an example to believers (vs. 7)
> Word of the Lord sounded forth from you (vs. 8)
> We need not say anything (vs. 8)
> They themselves report concerning us (vs. 9)
> You turned to God (vs. 9)

The movement of a passage can be readily observed when presented in this manner.

Another method of describing a passage is to make a simple outline. The first step is to divide the passage into paragraphs. Most of the recommended versions above have suggested paragraph breaks. The original text was not divided into paragraphs so you may want to divide it differently. Noticing changes of subject and natural divisions will help you determine the possible paragraph divisions. Looking at I Thessalonians 1, the passage could be divided in the following manner:

Paragraph I (vs. 1-5)
Paragraph II (vs. 6-10)

After determining your paragraph divisions, write a sentence or two summarizing each paragraph's contents. Don't worry if you omit important details, just give a general framework which you can fit the details into later. Notice the example below.

Passage Description: _____

> I Thessalonians 1
>
> vs. 1-5
>
>   After a word of greeting, Paul tells how thankful he is for the quality of life in the Thessalonian church
>
> vs. 6-10
>
>   In following Paul's example, the Thessalonians became a growing influence throughout Macedonia and Achaia. Everywhere people spoke about their response to God

How To Do Verse-By-Verse Meditation

The verse-by-verse meditation gives you an opportunity to make further observations and interpret the passage. At this point in the study you will take a prolonged look at the details as you proceed from one verse to the next verse. The Bible study essentials of observation, interpretation, correlation and application are also applied to the study of each individual *verse* as well as the entire passage.

The *STS* blank has three columns (Observations, Questions and Answers, Cross-references) for the three important aspects of verse-by-verse meditation. You can observe these in the completed *STS* blank on pages 42 and 43. You will also notice there is a narrow column on the left for the verse numbers.

Work across the page horizontally, not vertically! The objective is to meditate on the verse, not write something about every verse in every column. List the number in the left column. Then, take a concentrated look at this verse, noting on the blank your observations, questions, answers and cross-references. Space is provided for you to record additional information.

Observations

Proper observation is the foundation upon which good interpretation and application are built. As you focus on a verse, record your observations in the appropriate column. (You may want to review the section of observation in Unit I.)

Since it is impossible to record every observation in the space allotted, record the observations which stimulate you to further thinking. For example, I Thessalonians 1:2 says, "We give thanks to God always for you all, constantly mentioning you in our prayers." You might note "Paul thanked God for people." This could stimulate you to think "People are a gift from God." (Note: Since this is an interpretation made on the basis of observation, it should not be included in the observation column. You may wish to record this in your notes column on the far right of the *STS* blank.)

You will also want to record observations on the relationship of the specific verse to other verses in the passage. For example, in I Thessalonians 1:6, 7 you may observe that the Thessalonians were *followers* of some people and *examples* to others.

Questions

The "question" section takes considerable time and effort but it often leads to very rewarding meditations. As you grow in your knowledge of the Bible, you will have more questions — and they will be increasingly penetrating and significant. At the same time, your knowledge and understanding will increase.

Look at I Thessalonians 1:5, "for our gospel came to you not only in word, but also in power and in the Holy Spirit and with full conviction. You know what kind of men we proved to be among you for your sake." At first you may not have any questions. A closer look might cause you to ask:

"Are 'power,' 'in the Holy Spirit,' and 'in full conviction' three expressions which mean the same thing?"

"What manner of men were they among the Thessalonians?" (A cross-reference in Acts 17 may help answer this question.)

"Shouldn't Paul's motivation be for Jesus' glory rather than 'for your sake'?"

There is no limit to the number or variety of questions for any particular passage.

Answers

When a question has several possible answers, more than one can be recorded. The Scriptures do not provide clearcut answers for every issue, so be careful not to always insist on finding one. Major on what God has plainly revealed. Sometimes it is best to write your questions without trying to answer them. This allows you time to think about the questions. And, in some cases, a succeeding verse may answer your question. Waiting to answer some questions may keep you from pursuing unnecessary tangents.

In many cases, a question will stimulate further study in the Bible or in other sources. For example, I Corinthians 16:15 (KJV) speaks of men who have "addicted themselves to the ministry of the saints." The question "What are the characteristics of an addict?" may stimulate you to find an answer in a medical textbook.

In most cases, however, you will want to find as many answers as possible from the Word itself. Often a cross-reference will help you answer a question.

Cross-references

The Bible is its own best commentary. Scripture interprets Scripture. The content of one passage clarifies the content of another. There are two varieties of cross-references: internal and external. An internal cross-reference is located in the same book as the verse being studied. An external cross-reference comes from another portion of Scripture.

Internal cross-references show the relationship of a verse with the paragraph, the chapter and the book in which it is found. This type of cross-reference helps preserve the textual context of the verse.

Whenever a verse uses a connective word such as "wherefore," "and," "therefore," "hence," etc., an internal cross-reference will show what it refers to.

External cross-references show how the verse being studied relates to other verses in the Bible. It is especially noteworthy to find other writers who have said essentially the same thing. Some of the most important types of external cross-references are parallel, contrasting, corresponding and illustrative cross-references.

Parallel cross-references say virtually the same thing as the verse being studied but often add additional facts. For example, I Thessalonians 2:12, "to lead a life worthy of God, who calls you into His own Kingdom and glory" is similar to Ephesians 4:1, "I therefore, a prisoner for the Lord, beg you to lead a life worthy of the calling to which you have been called." While their content is similar, Ephesians 4:2,3 goes on to explain more fully how to walk in this manner.

Contrasting cross-references are verses which seem to contradict the verse being considered. For example, I Thessalonians 5:14 says to admonish idlers. II Thessalonians 3:6 says to keep aloof from every brother who leads an idle life. What is the difference? How can you do both? The new insight gained from the resolution of this seeming contradiction is one of the benefits of this type of cross-reference.

Corresponding cross-references are verses which either quote another verse from the Scriptures or refer to some event from Scripture. I Thessalonians 2:1 says, "For you yourselves know, brethren, that our visit to you was not in vain." Acts 17 describes Paul's visit and his actions among the Thessalonians.

Illustrative cross-references are the historical accounts which clearly illustrate a principle stated in Scripture. I Peter 5:8, "Be sober, be watchful. Your adversary the devil prowls around like a roaring lion, seeking some one to devour," illustrates the principle of sobriety and its importance in fighting your adversary the devil. This verse corresponds to I Thessalonians 5:8 which describes your weapons of warfare against Satan, "But, since we belong to the day, let us be sober, and put on the breastplate of faith and love, and for a helmet the hope of salvation."

A number of sources of cross-references are available. Many Bibles print references in the margins or in a concordance in the back of the Bible. If you are looking for a verse which contains a key word, don't hesitate to use a concordance. Don't, however, fall into the trap of relying on them completely rather than thinking for yourself.

The Treasury of Scripture Knowledge (Fleming H. Revell Co., Publishers) is a book which lists 500,000 cross-references covering every book of the Bible. It is another handy tool.

In the space next to the cross-reference add your linking thought — the thought that relates this cross-reference with the verse being studied. Use a short phrase or key words from the reference to help you retain its content.

Additional Notes

The blank column is provided for your own study emphasis. You may wish to title it with a specific topic or to list implications, possible applications, illustrations, definitions, etc.

How To Do the Theme and Conclusions

By the time you arrive at the theme and conclusion section of the *STS* Bible study you will have done a considerable amount of study. You will have described the passage, meditated on each verse, made observations, asked questions, discovered answers and found cross-references.

The theme is the central issue discussed by the writer. It may be a topic, a proposition, a problem or an argument. You may find more than one theme in a particular passage.

The best way to arrive at the theme is to ask yourself, "What is the author talking about?" or "What is the subject of each paragraph?" You can be sure that each paragraph has only one basic theme. Combining the paragraph themes will help determine the major theme of the passage.

After arriving at the theme or themes of the passage, begin to record the conclusions. In each paragraph there may be more than one conclusion because the author may be saying more than one thing about the subject.

The most accurate way to arrive at conclusions is to ask, "What is the author saying about the theme?" "What is being said about the topic or subject of each paragraph?" It is not as important to have a great number of conclusions as it is to have conclusions which capture the main themes running through the passage.

Here are some possible themes and conclusions from the two paragraphs in I Thessalonians 1:

Theme: *Paul's Gospel in Thessalonica (vs 1-5)*
Paul's Effective Ministry in Thessalonica (vs. 6-10)

Conclusions: *Prayer, preaching and the demonstration of power are three keys to communicating the Gospel (vs. 2, 5)*
An effective Gospel ministry includes being imitators to some and examples to others (vs. 6, 7)
Turning to God from idols is a work of faith, serving a living God is a labor of love and waiting for His Son is steadfastness of hope (vs. 3, 9, 10)

34

How To Write an Application

Bible study without application leads to vain knowledge. Knowledge is only in the mind while application is in the life.

"The Scriptures were not given to increase our knowledge but to change our lives."   D.L. Moody

---

Recording your application will help you clarify what you plan to do. It also encourages you to be specific. It is easy to say, "I am going to pray more." That type of application is seldom put into practice. It is far more meaningful to write down, "I am going to spend the first five minutes of my lunch break each day in prayer."

The following four questions may help you write meaningful applications.

"What is the truth I want to apply?"

"What is my need?"

"What is my plan of action?"

"How can I check my progress?"

Here is a possible application from I Thessalonians 1:

Application: The truth of I Thess. 1:9 is to turn from idols and focus on Christ.

My need results from making money my idol. I hold on too tightly to my paycheck and possessions and am selfish with how I spend what God has given.

I will plan to draw up a budget this week and give at least 10% to Christ's work. I will also memorize I Thess. 1:9,10

I will check myself by sharing my application with my roommate and having him review my verses with me.

35

How To Do
A Book Summary

To complete your study of a book you will need to tie together what you have learned in a book summary. Your book summary will help you unify knowledge, consolidate facts and grasp the whole book.

The first step in the book summary is to reread the book several times. Each time you reread the book, do it in one sitting. Since you are now well acquainted with the material you should be able to read it rapidly. Look for the movement of the book — the general thread that runs through it. Try to get an overall view of the book.

Reviewing your chapter titles will help you determine the general flow of the book. From your titles and major breakdowns, write an outline for the whole book. It is interesting to compare your final outline with your book overview on the *Survey Blank*.

Next review your passage themes and major conclusions. Decide which theme or themes are most important and list them on the *Summary Blank*. Now do the same thing with your conclusions, choosing the most crucial ones and listing them on the blank.

Consider the book as a whole and give it a title. Try to keep your titles short and use words that are picturesque or illustrative of the book's contents.

Finally, review your applications for each passage. Are there any applications you haven't completed yet? From your review write out your final application and make definite plans to complete it.

A sample *Book Summary* can be found on page 39.

STS Book Survey

Book _I Thess._   Date _9-10-74_

Principal Personalities: _Paul, the author; Timothy and Silas (Silvanus), co-workers with Paul while he ministered to the Thessalonians_

Historical Setting: _Paul, Silas and Timothy went about 100 miles southwest of Philippi to Thessalonica (Acts 17) They spent about three weeks there and a growing church was begun. Paul probably wrote this letter after his visit while in Athens (A.D. 52) This is the earliest of Paul's epistles._

Purpose: _To help overcome problems with Paul's character and ministry, to instruct on the doctrine of the return of Christ and to encourage them while they were being persecuted_

Themes: _The Second Coming of Christ_
Paul's Personal Ministry
Purity of Life

Style: _Personal, reminiscent, instructional_
Key Words: _God the Father, Jesus Christ, Holy Spirit, Faith, Love, Hope, Joy_
Additional Personalities: _no more mentioned_

Geography: _Thessalonica was the capitol of Macedonia on the commercial trade route. It became a free city after the battle of Phillipi (42 BC)_

Overview: _____

I. Personal - Paul's past and present dealings
with the Thessalonian church (Chapters 1-3)
A. Greeting (1:1)
B. Thanksgiving (1:2-10)
C. The ministry of the apostles (2:1-20)
  1. As evangelists (2:1-6)
  2. As pastors (2:7-9)
  3. As teachers (2:10-12)
  4. The result of the apostles' ministry (2:13-16)
  5. Satanic opposition to the ministry (2:17-18)
  6. The reward of the ministry (2:19,20)
D. Timothy's report as to the progress of
the church (3:1-13)
  1. Timothy sent to Thessalonica (3:1-5)
  2. Timothy brings back good tidings
  of the Thessalonians (3:6-13)
II. Practical - Instruction concerning the life
Christians should live in view of the
immediate return of the Lord (Chapters 4,5)
A. Instruction regarding holiness (4:1-8)
B. Instruction regarding love of brethren (4:9,10)
C. Instruction regarding conduct towards
those outside the church (4:11,12)
D. Instruction regarding the rapture of
the saints
E. Instruction regarding the revelation
of Christ (5:14)
F. Sundry instructions (5:12-28)

_____

(From The Bible Book by Book by G. Coleman Luck, Moody
Press.)

STS Book Summary

Book _I Thessalonians_ Date _10-20-74_

Book Title: _"A Way of Life for New Christians"_

Final Outline:

I. The Effects of the Gospel on the Thessalonians (1:1-10).

II. Paul's Personal Ministry to the Thessalonians (2:1-20).

III. God's Purpose for the Lives of the Thessalonians (3:1- 4:12)

IV. Expectation for the Return of Christ (4:13-18).

V. A Challenge to a Changed Life for the Thessalonians (5:1-28).

Major Theme(s): _The hope of Christ's return inspires_
(1:8-10), rewards (2:17-20), purifies (4:1-12), com-
forts (4:13-18) and awakens to action (5:1-10).
    Faith produces work (1:3,9) love
produces labor (1:3,9) and hope produces
patience (1:3,10).
    The purpose of afflictions is to
produce sanctification in the believer
_(1:6; 2:14-16; 3:1-10; 5:1-10)._

Major Conclusions: _____
    The hope of Christ's return permeates
all a Christian's beliefs.
    Faith, hope and love are to
be the model attitudes and sparks
to action.
    Afflictions are not to be feared,
but enjoyed as sources of growth
and development.

Final Application: _I want to memorize all_
the verses in I Thessalonians
that relate to encouraging others
with hope (2:19,20; 3:11-13; 4:15-18;
5:9,11), and to begin to share these truths
with others, beginning with my room-
mate who's a new Christian.

Search the Scriptures

Passage _I Thessalonians 1_ Date _9-17-74_

Passage Description: _____

    I Thessalonians 1

    vs. 1-5

      After a word of greeting, Paul tells
how thankful he is for the quality
of life in the Thessalonian church.

    vs. 6-10

      In following Paul's example, the
Thessalonians became a growing
influence throughout Macedonia and
Achaia. Everywhere people spoke
about their response to God.

Verse by Verse Meditation

Vs.	Observation:	Vs.	Questions and Answers (Interpretation)
1	A letter from 3 men who probably traveled together	1	When were they in Thessalonica?
2	Paul gives thanks for them (denotes his personal concern)	2	What did Paul pray for them? (Eph. 1:17-21; 3:16-21)
3	Three parallel thoughts: 1. work of faith 2. labor of love 3. steadfastness of hope	3	What is faith? Trusting in God's character & obeying Him. What is steadfastness of hope? "Patient waiting for Christ, enduring trials until He comes."*
4	God chose me!	4	When did God choose me?
5	Gospel can be communicated through a. power b. Holy Spirit c. full conviction	5	What is conviction? "Describes the willingness and freedom of Spirit enjoyed by those who brought Gospel to Thess."**
6	They were imitators of Paul	6	Whom are we to imitate?
7	They were examples to "all" Greece (note contrast)	7	
8	"Word" mentioned also vs. 5, 6. Faith is directed toward God. Faith always has an object. Macedonia & Achaia were the regions of their ministry	8	Where is Macedonia? Achaia? North of Greece, M. was conquered by Rome in 168 B.C. Achaia was divided from M. in 140 B.C.***
9	Ministry had 3 effects: 1. turned to God from idols 2. served living God 3. Wait for Son from heaven	9	Was idol worship a common practice?
10	Christ's resurrection is linked with His Coming again	10	Is resurrection commonly linked with Second Coming?

© The Navigators 1974
* Unger's Bible Handbook ** Vine's Expository Dictionary
*** Unger's Bible Dictionary

Vs.	Cr. Ref. and Linking Thought (Correlation)		Notes & Comments
1	Acts 17:1	After they visited Amphipolis & Apollonia	Maybe I should write Joe a follow-up letter
2	1 Thess 5:18	Give thanks in everything	- do topical study on thanksgiving
3	II Thess 3:5	Steadfastness of Christ	Am I enduring under trials? Am I focus-ing on Christ as my hope?
	Heb 11:1	Faith is confident assurance of the unseen & future	
4	II Thess 2:13	From the beginning	Do I really know how to explain the Gospel? Need to work on memo-rizing a simple plan of salvation.
5	Col 2:2	Full assurance or conviction of under-standing results in knowing Christ	
6	1 Cor. 11:1	Follow me as I follow Christ	How can I be a better example?
8	Acts 16:9	Paul had a vision to go to Macedonia	What is my faith directed toward?
9	Acts 19:19	Ephesians burned their idols and magic books	Am I worshipping any idols?
10	I Thess 4: 16, 17	Links resurrection with Second Coming	

Title: The Gospel and Paul's Effective
Ministry in Thessalonica

Theme: Paul's Gospel in Thessalonica (vs. 1-5)
Paul's Effective Ministry in Thessalonica
(vs. 6-10)

Conclusions: Prayer, preaching and the
demonstration of power are three keys to
communicating the Gospel (vs. 2, 5)
    An effective Gospel ministry includes
being imitators to some and examples to others (vs. 6, 7)
    Turning to God from idols is a work
of faith, serving a living God is a labor
of love and waiting for His Son is
steadfastness of hope (vs. 3, 9, 10)

Application: The truth of I Thess. 1:9 is to turn from
idols and focus on Christ.
    My need results from making money my
idol. I hold on too tightly to my paycheck and
possessions and am selfish with how I
spend what God has given.
    I will plan to draw up a budget this
week and give at least 10% to Christ's work.
I will also memorize I Thess. 1:9, 10
    I will check myself by sharing my application
with my roommate and having him review my
verses with me.

Summary:
Unit Two

The Approach

1. There are three steps to the *STS* chapter analysis Bible study method:
   a. The passage description (whole)
   b. Verse-by-verse meditation (particulars)
   c. Theme and conclusion (conclusions)
2. Application can be drawn from any of these steps.

The Book Survey

1. Research principal personalities and historical setting.
2. Determine the purpose and the theme.
3. Summarize in chart, outline or a diagram.

Chapter Analysis

1. Describe the passage in an outline, paraphrase, etc.
2. Do a verse-by-verse meditation:
   a. Record observations.
   b. Ask yourself questions and find the answers if possible.
   c. Use internal and external cross-references and tie them together with linking thoughts.
   d. Record any additional notes.
3. Draw together themes and conclusions.
4. Record your application.

Book Summary

1. Reread the book several times looking for general movement.
2. Review chapter titles and write a book outline.
3. Review passage themes and major conclusions, recording the most important ones on the *Summary Blank*.
4. Give the book a title.
5. Review your applications and complete them.

Unit Three:
Improving Your
Bible Study Skills

Introduction

Unit III will help you improve the skills that you have already learned and launch you into developing your own methods of doing Bible study. Before you use the methods here, make sure you are familiar with the methods described in Unit II of this booklet. After you have done Bible study for a few weeks using that method, refer to this unit.

The contents of this unit follow the general format of the *STS* method (Passage Description, Observation, Verse-by-verse Meditation, Theme and Conclusions, Application). As you begin to sense the need for some additional help in a particular part of your Bible study, refer to the appropriate section.

This section will teach you new concepts of Bible study as well as new methods. Take sufficient time to thoroughly understand any new concepts. You will want to employ these in all of the methods you use.

The methods in this unit are only a sampling of the hundreds that are available. Use your creativity to develop new methods, but before you do, take time to learn the methods presented. True creativity follows structure.

Passage Description

Feel free to be creative in your description of passages. An easy and effective means of describing a passage is the vertical chart. The first step in making a vertical chart is to divide the chapter into paragraphs. Mark down the beginning verse and ending verse of each paragraph on your chart. For example, in I Thessalonians 1 there are two paragraphs, verses 1-5 and verses 6-10.

I THESSALONIANS 1	
PARAGRAPH 1 : VS. 1 - 5 VS. I VS. 5	PARAGRAPH 2 : VS. 6 - 10 VS. 6 VS. 10

The next step is to write in key thoughts from the paragraph in the block allotted for the paragraph. Avoid interpretation at this point.

I THESSALONIANS 1	

PARAGRAPH 1 : VS. 1 - 5
VS. I - Paul greets the
    Thessalonians
  - prays
  - brought Gospel
 	
VS. 5
	PARAGRAPH 2 : VS. 6 - 10
	VS. 6 - The Thessalonians :
	  - became imitators
	  - became examples
	  - faith spread abroad
	  - turned to God
	VS. 10

49

The third step is to title your paragraphs. Consider the key thoughts you have in your chart rather than rereading the biblical text. From this example consider the thoughts from the first paragraph. One title for this paragraph is "The Gospel Received." Other possibilities might be "Paul's Ministry" or "The Enlivening Message."

I THESSALONIANS 1	
GOSPEL RECEIVED	*GOSPEL RESULTS*
PARAGRAPH 1 : VS. 1 – 5 *VS.1 – Paul greets the Thessalonians* *– prays* *– brought Gospel* *VS.5*	*PARAGRAPH 2 : VS. 6 – 10* *VS.6 – The Thessalonians :* *– became imitators* *– became examples* *– faith spread abroad* *– turned to God* *VS.10*

Personal Paraphrase

Another form of passage description is the paraphrase — stating the content of the passage in contemporary language. Some modern "translations" provide good examples of a paraphrase. The following excerpts are from *The New Testament in Modern English* by J.B. Phillips and *The Living Bible* by Kenneth Taylor.

(I Thessalonians 2:7,8 — Phillips)

"Our attitude among you was one of tenderness, rather like that of a devoted nurse among her babies. Because we loved you, it was a joy to us to give you not only the gospel of God but our very hearts — so dear had you become to us."

(I Thessalonians 2:7,8 — Living)

"But we were as gentle among you as a mother feeding and caring for her own children. We loved you dearly — so dearly at we gave you not only God's message, but our own lives too."

While being creative in your personal paraphrasing, do not stray from the basic content of the passage.

Detailed Outline

Some people enjoy using a detailed outline for their passage description. This type of outline includes every idea mentioned in the passage without omitting any details. A detailed outline of I Thessalonians 1:1-5 appears below:

I. PAUL'S GREETING (1:1)

    A. From: Paul, Silvanus & Timothy

    B. To: The church of the Thessalonians in God & Christ

    C. Greeting: Grace to you & peace

II. PAUL'S PRAYER AND GOSPEL MINISTRY (1:2-5)

    A. Paul's prayer for the Thessalonians (vs. 2,3)

       1. Always giving thanks for them

       2. Constantly remembering their:

          a. Work of faith

          b. Labor of love   } in Christ in the presence of God

          c. Steadfastness of hope

    B. Paul's Gospel Ministry to the Thessalonians (vs. 4-5)

       1. God loved the Thessalonians & chose them

       2. The Gospel came:

          a. In Word

          b. In power

          c. In the Holy Spirit

          d. With full conviction

       3. Paul's manner of living was for their sake

Creative Approaches

You can incorporate many creative approaches into your passage description as long as you include the content of the passage without interpreting it. Here are two examples of a creative approach to I Thessalonians 1:

The Macedonian Herald

FINAL EDITION   **1 DENARIUS**

Thessalonica (U.P.) - Word today reached Macedonia concerning a mysterious happening in Thessalonica. After the arrival of an itinerant preacher by the name of Paul, the Thessalonians are exhibiting strange behavior. They have turned from idols to "serve God" and to wait for His Son to return from Heaven. "God's son," known by the name of Jesus, was reported several years ago to have been raised from death. He is also said to have power to deliver people from the "judgement" which is to come.

The message preached by Paul seems to have been accompanied by power and full conviction, for there is no other way to explain the response of the Thessalonians.

Paul has left Thessalonica, but it is reported that he continues to pray for the Thessalonians, remembering their work of faith, labor of love and steadfastness of hope.

Observation

The essential of observation applies to every aspect of your Bible study. Observation is included in every phase of the *STS* study method so that it becomes a pervading attitude and skill for effective Bible study.

Have the Right Mental Attitude

You have already learned that two basic requirements for making good observations are the attitudes of an open mind and an open life. As you have worked on making good observations, you have probably become aware that more is required than just these two attitudes. Five more requirements are listed below.

1. *Observation requires an act of the will.* You must have the will and the desire to be aware and to perceive and recognize. There must be the will to know and to learn. For example, when you meet people for the first time, do you remember their names? If not, it is likely that you have not purposed in your mind that you are going to learn their names. Learning begins with an act of the will.

2. *Observation requires a persistence to know.* Learning is never easy. It requires diligence and discipline. There is no such thing as an effective disciple without discipline. One of the keys in persisting in your Bible study is to see that the results are really worth the effort and the work that it takes. Take time to reflect on the results that have taken place in your life over the past six months because of Bible study.

3. *Observation requires patience.* In a day when you have instant coffee, instant communication, instant everything, there is a tendency to want an instant education. It takes a great deal of time to learn. There are no short cuts in the learning process. The so-called short cuts are in fact only short circuits; they lead to ineffective results. In Bible study as well as in everything else in the Christian life, the process is as important as the product.

4. *Observation requires diligent recording.* Take a moment right now to review one of the Bible study blanks you worked on six months ago. As you look over the observations you recorded, you will notice that there are some you have forgotten about. There will be only a small portion that you remember. So jot down your observations diligently. (Once again you see the importance and value of having a study Bible where you can keep a record of your good observations for the next time you study.)

5. *Observation requires caution.* Observation is the first step in studying the Bible, but it is not the whole of Bible study. Three warnings are appropriate:

1. Don't lose yourself in the details, but divide your time proportionately.

2. Don't stop with observations, but go on to ask questions, get answers, etc.

3. Don't give equal weight to everything, but discern what is most important.

Consider Comparisons and Contrasts

Two of the things to look for in your Bible study are *comparisons and contrasts.* Comparisons show how two things are alike. Contrasts show how two things differ. Make a special effort to find comparisons and contrasts in the passage. If there are none in the passage, try to find other Scriptures which will give you

comparison

contrast and comparisons with the section you are studying.

Make sure to take careful notice of words like "even so," "as ... so ...," "likewise ...". These are not the only times you will find comparisons, but they almost always give a comparison. When you find a comparison, spend sufficient time meditating on what two things are being compared. Think of as many ways as possible they are alike.

Contrasts may be more difficult to find because the range of intensity can vary from distinct contrasts to mild differences. Look for things which are similar in one respect and dissimilar in another. Key words to look for are "but," "nor," and "not."

Here especially you will want to use cross-references. As you read a story or a statement in the Scriptures, consider things which are similar in certain respects, but different in others. Observing these contrasts will help you discern the overall truth of the Word.

In I Thessalonians 2 two comparisons are made between Paul's ministry and the role of parents with children. In verse 7 he is compared to "a nursing mother" (NASB) and in verse 11 he is described as " ... exhorting and encouraging and imploring each one of you as a father .. " (NASB). Considering the characteristics of a mother you might think about infant care—tenderness, caring for them individually, feeding them, etc. Considering the role of a father you might think about discipline, concern, teaching and giving direction. Considering these thoughts will give you ad-

contrast

55

ditional insight into Paul's character and relationship to the Thessalonians.

Several contrasts also appear in this chapter—"not as pleasing men *but* God..." (verse 4, NASB); "we were well pleased to impart to you *not only* the Gospel of God, *but also* our own lives" (verse 8, NASB).

Be Sensitive to Form and Structure

As you observe the contents of the passage, you'll also want to become aware of the form it takes. How God says something is as important as what He says. How does the author deal with the content? What form or structure does it take?

For example, you may notice:

"He asks four questions and answers them."

"In this passage the writer lists seventeen commands to obey."

"In this passage, the writer makes three declarative statements and then supports them."

The form of content may be poetry, narrative, parable, logic, discourse, practice, history, drama, etc. The way that the content of Scripture unfolds reveals the mind and method of the writer, and can give you insight into the feeling and the meaning of the passage.

Some other things to look for as you examine structure are:

1. Use of cause and effect (as in I Thessalonians 1).
2. The movement from particulars to generalities (as in I Thessalonians 2), or from generalities to particulars (as in I Thessalonians 5).
3. Use of Old Testament references in the New Testament.
4. Use of illustrations in the text of Scripture.
5. Use of the current events of the times.

Notice Proportions

The law of proportions is one of the keys to maintaining a balance of emphasis in your Bible study. Make sure that you are observing proportion. There is proportion in terms of importance, people, time and subject matter. For example, the following chart of the Book of Acts will help you observe the proportion of time throughout the book.

Chapters	1	2	3-8	9-12	13,14	15	16- 18:22	18:23 21:16	21:17- 28
Time Span	50 days	1 day	2 years	9 years	1½ years	few days	2½ years	4 years	5 years

The Book of Acts

In the Book of I Thessalonians, notice how much of the text deals with the Second Coming of Christ. Also notice how much reference Paul made to his unblamable conduct and behavior before the Thessalonians. These proportionate observations can give you a clue to Paul's major emphases in writing this epistle.

Record Repetitions

As you do your Bible study, take particular note to see what words, phrases and expressions are repeated.

You can make a little diagram for yourself like this:

WORD OR PHRASE	NUMBER OF REPETITIONS	VERSES USED
FAITH	5	2,5,6,7,10
AFFLICTION	3	3,4,7

The chart is partially filled in from repetitions found in I Thessalonians 3. The benefit of this method is not in filling out the chart. Seeing repetition is only an observation that leads you to asking the right questions.

Noticing that the word "faith" appears five times, you might ask, "Why is faith mentioned so often?" "What is faith linked with in this chapter?" "What increases faith?" Seeing the repetition of "affliction," you might conclude "faith is increased by the right response to affliction."

In almost every passage you will study there will be words or phrases that will be repeated. Look for them and take note of them. Determine why they are repeated and how they are related.

Observation also includes the opposite aspect of repetition — omission. As you study the passage, think to yourself, "What words or phrases or ideas would I include in this passage?" If these thoughts and ideas are omitted, why are they omitted? Is there a substitute in their place? What is the substitute? It is much more difficult to see omissions than it is to see repetitions. But omissions should be carefully noted.

For example, a very notable omission occurs in the Book of Acts. The word love isn't mentioned in the entire book. On the other hand, the ideas of unity and oneness are repeated often.

Visualize the Verbs

One of the keys to making good observations is to note the action of a passage. Action is carried by verbs. They tell us what is being done.

Try to underline all of the verbs in the passage that you are studying. (There is a very good loose-leaf New Testament available from the American Bible Society. It has wide margins and is excellent for Bible study.) You may want to list these verbs on your study blank.

After you have gone through and underlined all of the verbs, examine what you have underlined. What kind of action is there? Are most of the verbs passive? Is the subject influenced or acted upon rather than active itself? Do the verbs indicate that the passage is basically narrative? Are there any quotations? Are the verbs imperative — do they make commands? Which verbs are repeated? What is the significance of this?

After you have answered these questions, take another look at these verbs. There must be something else that you haven't seen yet. Remember, observation is the first step of all good Bible study.

Picture the Illustrations

Have you ever been struck by now many verbal illustrations there are in the Bible? Many of the writers that God used in providing His Word talked in pictures. Jesus used this device often. He called His followers vines, sheep, fishermen, farmers, etc. Pay particular attention to finding illustrations in the passage you are studying. Some illustrations are very obvious like the vine in John 15. Others are not so obvious, but the Scriptures abound with illustrations and word pictures. In James 3 alone, there are at least nine different illustrations.

Once you notice an illustration, meditate on how the illustration clarifies the subject of the passage. Also ask what other illustrations are used to present this subject. Now you can compare and contrast your illustration. For example, in I Thessalonians 5:2, a thief in the night illustrates the need for being prepared; in I Thessalonians 5:3, a woman with child illustrates suddenness; in I Thessalonians 5:8, a breastplate of faith illustrates being equipped.

If there are no illustrations given in a passage you are studying (highly unlikely), look for illustrations and examples in other portions of Scripture relevant to the subject of the passage you are studying.

Examine the Explanations

An explanation is anything that is used to illustrate, clarify, illuminate, describe or demonstrate. An explanation may be one verse long or a whole chapter.

To clearly understand an explanation, you must follow the logic of the writer. What point is he trying to make? How is he trying to make it? How does he present his point?

Sometimes the Scriptures explain a question that is not stated but implied. Often a statement in a verse will cause you to ask a question and the following verse will answer your question. Be sure to note this type of tie between verses or paragraphs. For example, Romans 3:28 says "For we hold that a man is justified by faith apart from works of law." A natural question which may result from meditation on the verse is "Could people in the Old Testament be saved?"

A few verses later in Romans 4, Paul explains how Abraham and David were both justified by faith without the deeds of the law. This helps explain Romans 3:28. Do not, however, presume that these portions of Scripture in Chaper 4 were written primarily to explain Romans 3:28.

Change Your Viewpoint

To change your viewpoint you will have to eliminate preconceived ideas. Do not allow these to control or even to color your thinking about the Word of God. Read the verse as though you were someone else. In I Thessalonians 2:14-16, Paul levels several accusations at a particular group of people. You might envision these people as vicious and cruel. The fact is that this group was well respected and accepted in their society. With this in mind, change your viewpoint and reread this passage making new observations.

One of the more interesting ways to change your viewpoint is to put yourself in another person's shoes. How would you feel if you were the author of this epistle? How would you as a recipient understand the message? What would a third party at the scene, like Timothy, think of the situation as he listened to Paul? From a strict Jewish point of view, react to Paul's point of view. Learn to observe from a different perspective.

The above are only a few methods of making observations. You can list many more methods of discovering what is being said by the author. The preceding list is only meant to be a stimulator for further study. Take the liberty to add to the list as you discover more techniques for observing the text.

Verse-by-verse Meditation

Verse-by-verse meditation will require a major amount of your personal study time. Don't rush. Thoughtfully, prayerfully, look into all the nooks and crannies of the passage. Envision yourself on a treasure hunt — leaving no stone unturned.

Defining Important Words

While Webster's dictionary is very helpful in defining the English words of a Bible passage, it is inadequate in giving the literal meanings of Hebrew or Greek words or phrases. To check the definition of a biblical word, the average person must rely on other resources. Often a Bible dictionary will give a more thorough and comprehensive description of a word or topic. Using James Strong's *Exhaustive Concordance of the Bible* or *Young's Analytical Concordance to the Bible* will help you find the actual Hebrew or Greek words used in a passage. These particular books also give brief definitions of the particular words, but a Hebrew or Greek lexicon will give you further insights.

Other background material which will prove very helpful in defining New Testament words are W.E. Vine's *An Expository Dictionary of New Testament Words* and M.R. Vincent's *Word Studies in the New Testament*. Girdlestone's *Old Testament Synonyms* is a good reference for Old Testament word studies. Good commentaries, explaining the literal meaning of biblical words and phrases, will also be helpful. Thus, without a command of either the Hebrew or Greek languages, you can profit in your study of the Scriptures from the excellent scholarship and research available in a few well chosen books.

Questions and Answers

It has been said that it is as important to have the right questions as it is to have the right answers — so it is with Bible study. Thorough study of a passage of Scripture is not complete without bombarding the text with questions — questions you have, questions others may have, simple as well as difficult questions.

Why question the Scriptures? Consider the following reasons:

1. Carefully writing out questions helps you clarify what is unknown. It is easy to say, "I don't understand verse five." As you write good questions, you will define exactly what is not known or understood. It is the truly educated man who knows what he does not know.

Questions which reflect what is not known are not trivial. Consider I Thessalonians 1:4, "Knowing, brethren beloved, your election of God" (KJV). Only asking "What does election mean?" is poor. You are more likely to discover answers for yourself by also asking questions like:

> "What was the election of the Thessalonians?"
> "Does election refer to salvation?"
> "When does election take place for a believer?"

2. Questions help you discover what assumptions are being made. Questioning what seems obvious often helps establish the truth. This deepens biblical convictions and helps keep you from being dogmatic about areas where Scripture is inconclusive.

There is profit in asking questions when you think you "know" the answer. You may be surprised to discover you cannot verbalize an accurate answer. For example, while studying I Thessalonians 1:5 you might ask, "What is the Gospel?" This is far from a trivial question.

3. Questions open up a wealth of material for meditation. Many questions have more than one answer — or they do not have a conclusive answer. Asking questions of this kind automatically focuses your mind on possible answers which can be extremely profitable for meditation. Good resources for this type of question are illustrations, contrasts and comparisons.

For example, in I Thessalonians 5:8 Paul compares the hope of salvation with a helmet. There are several answers to the question, "How is salvation like a helmet?" Meditating on this question may help you understand salvation in a new way.

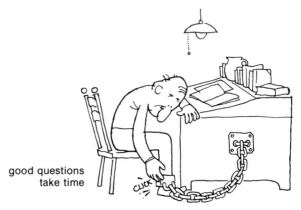

good questions
take time

Cross-references

The best commentary on the Bible is the Bible. Cross-references will help you discover the continuity of the Bible and how God has progressively revealed His truth.

Have cross-references been a drag or a joy for you?

When cross-referencing becomes mechanical it is an indication that you are trying to find cross-references in order to meet a quota or to fill out a blank. Remember the objective is to *study the Bible*, not do a Bible study!

Review the types of cross-references listed in Unit II. Now review last week's Bible study. How many of each type of cross-reference did you use? Are you getting into a rut? Are you using one type of cross-reference predominately?

Take time right now to think about other types of cross-references you can use. List some on a sheet of paper. This week make a special effort to use some of these new types of cross-references.

Spend time thinking about the cross-references you jot down. It is far better to have five meaningful cross-references listed for an entire passage than it is to have five cross-references for each verse if you have not thought about them.

Theme and Conclusions

The theme and conclusions section is the place to develop your study into concrete statements of faith. Thought chains and topical grids are two methods which will help you determine the correct theme and make valid conclusions.

How to Make a Thought Chain

Thought chains graphically associate similar ideas. You will need a study Bible you can mark in and some colored pencils. Look through a passage for similar thoughts. Then using one color for similar ideas, draw a circle around each one. Using the same color, connect the circles with thin lines and give the chain a title. Use different colors to make other chains of associated thoughts.

Now consider chain titles to see how they fit together to make one theme for the passage. In the example on the next page only one chain has been worked out. It is the "Character of the Minister." Other chains might be titled "Effect of the Ministry" and "Concern for Young Christians." These lead to the theme, "How to Minister to Young Believers."

THE FIRST LETTER OF PAUL
TO THE
THESSALONIANS

1 Paul, Silva'nus, and Timothy,
To the church of the Thessalo'nians in God the Father and the Lord Jesus Christ:
Grace to you and peace.

2 We give thanks to God always for you all, constantly mentioning you in our prayers, 3 remembering before our God and Father your work of faith and labor of love and steadfastness of hope in our Lord Jesus Christ. 4 For we know, brethren beloved by God, that he has chosen you; 5 for our gospel came to you not only in word, but also in power and in the Holy Spirit and with full conviction. You know what kind of men we proved to be among you for your sake. 6 And you became imitators of us and of the Lord, for you received the word in much affliction, with joy inspired by the Holy Spirit; 7 so that you became an example to all the believers in Macedo'nia and in Acha'ia. 8 For not only has the word of the Lord sounded forth from you in Macedo'nia and Acha'ia, but your faith in God has gone forth everywhere, so that we need not say anything. 9 For they themselves report concerning us what a welcome we had among you, and how you turned to God from idols, to serve a living and true God, 10 and to wait for his Son from heaven, whom he raised from the dead, Jesus who delivers us from the wrath to come.

2 For you yourselves know, brethren, that our visit to you was not in vain; 2 but though we had already suffered and been shamefully treated at Philippi, as you know, we had courage in our God to declare to you the gospel of God in the face of great opposition. 3 For our appeal does not spring from error or uncleanness, nor is it made with guile; 4 but just as we have been approved by God to be entrusted with the gospel, so we speak, not to please men,

352

but to please God who tests our hearts. For we never used either words of flattery, as you know, or a cloak for greed, as God is witness; 6 nor did we seek glory from men, whether from you or from others, though we might have made demands as apostles of Christ. 7 But we were gentle among you, like a nurse taking care of her children. 8 So, being affectionately desirous of you, we were ready to share with you not only the gospel of God but also our own selves, because you had become very dear to us. 9 For you remember our labor and toil, brethren; we worked night and day, that we might not burden any of you, while we preached to you the gospel of God. 10 You are witnesses, and God also, how holy and righteous and blameless was our behavior to you believers; 11 for you know how, like a father with his children, we exhorted each one of you and encouraged you and charged you 12 to lead a life worthy of God, who calls you into his own kingdom and glory. 13 And we also thank God constantly for this,

that when you received the word of God which you heard from us, you accepted it not as the word of men but as what it really is, the word of God, which is at work in you believers. 14 For you, brethren, became imitators of the churches of God in Christ Jesus which are in Judea; for you suffered the same things from your own countrymen as they did from the Jews, 15 who killed both the Lord Jesus and the prophets, and drove us out, and displease God and oppose all men 16 by hindering us from speaking to the Gentiles that they may be saved—so as always to fill up the measure of their sins. But God's wrath has come upon them at last!

17 But since we were bereft of you, brethren, for a short time, in person not in heart, we endeavored the more eagerly and with great desire to see you face to face; 18 because we wanted to come to you—I, Paul, again and again—but Satan hindered us. 19 For what is our hope or joy or crown of boasting before our Lord Jesus at his coming? Is it not you? 20 For you are our glory and joy.

a Other ancient authorities read babes
b Or completely, or for ever

(Handwritten annotation: CHARACTER OF THE MINISTER)

Each chain should also lead to one or more conclusions concerning the theme. In the chain of this example, it was noted that the character of the minister is both courageous and humble (not seeking glory). Hence, the conclusion: "Ministers ought to be humble and meek in attitude but bold and forceful in actions." In this manner continue to arrive at further conclusions. The thought chains will point to the subject of the passage — the major theme. Your conclusions are what is said about the major theme.

Be sure not to draw your lines prematurely. You will want to search the text more than once looking for elements of the same chain. Remember, making chains is not studying the Bible. It is a method to help you visualize in a different way what was already there.

64

How to Use a Topical Grid

There are many passages in the Scriptures which are clearly about one particular topic. For example, I Corinthians 13 is about love, I Corinthians 15 about the resurrection, II Peter 2 about false teachers. The theme of these chapters is usually best stated in a word or phrase, rather than a sentence.

In studying these passages a topical grid will help you arrive at good conclusions. A topical grid looks like this:

TOPIC: *Follow-up*　　　　CHAPTER: *I Thess. 2*

VS.	POSITIVE CHARACTERISTICS	NEGATIVE ATTITUDES	RELATIONSHIPS	ACTIVITIES
4	approved by God; entrusted with Gospel	not speaking to please men		
5		no flattering speech; not greedy		
6		no glory-seeking; not asserting authority		
7	gentle		a nursing mother	caring for them
8	having fond affection; very dear to them			imparting lives

In the left hand column put down the references that will break the chapter up into smaller portions. The smaller portions may be paragraphs, sentences or individual verses.

Next, determine what you want to investigate about this topic. These must be general categories, not specific questions. For example, if you are studying I Thessalonians 2 on follow-up, you may wish to find out:

What are the positive characteristics of the people doing the follow-up?

What are some negative attitudes to avoid in follow-up?

What are some of the relationships in follow-up?

What are some of the activities involved in follow-up?

These become the titles of your vertical columns. Now you simply work horizontally through the chart. That is, examine the first verse for characteristics, works, teachings, etc. Sometimes you will not have anything to record in a square. Don't try to twist the Scriptures to fit your grid. Record only what applies.

Once you have completed the grid, read it vertically. You would conclude from a study of I Thessalonians 2, using this chart, "the characteristics of people doing follow-up are...", "the negative attitudes to avoid are...", etc. You will want to record these conclusions on your *STS* blank.

How to Organize Your Study

One way of organizing the main points of your study is to use a horizontal chart. It graphically illustrates the relationship of the important ideas of your verse-by-verse meditation to your theme and conclusions. I Thessalonians 1 is illustrated below.

FINAL TITLE:
"PAUL'S EFFECTIVE MINISTRY"

Paragraph Titles

GOSPEL'S CAUSES	GOSPEL'S EFFECTS
Praying always	Became imitators
Work of faith	Received the Word
Labor of love	Became examples of faith
Steadfastness of hope	Turned to God
Election of God	Serve a living God
Holy Spirit	Wait for His Son
Example of men	
1 5	6 10

Theme — GOSPEL RECEIVED | GOSPEL RESULTS

Conclusions

Prayer, preaching and the demonstration of power are three keys to communicating the Gospel.	An effective ministry includes being imitators of some and examples to others.

Turning to God from idols is a work of faith, serving a living God is a labor of love, and waiting for His Son is steadfastness of hope.

66

Each section on the chart contains a paragraph. The paragraph divisions are indicated by the verse numbers in the corners. Write your paragraph titles at the top of each section. Then list the key thoughts that led you to your theme and conclusions under the titles. You may want to tie related thoughts together with arrows. Finally, record your theme and conclusions in the bottom section of the chart.

If you plan to use horizontal charts to organize each chapter of a book, you may wish to put all of your charts together on one piece of paper. This will result in one long chart which represents the main thoughts of the entire book. Often such a representation will enable you to understand the book as a whole.

Application

Good application questions are difficult. This section will provide you with some stimulating ideas about new areas of application and how to overcome hindrances.

Possible Areas of Application

There are at least seven areas of your life in which you can make applications. The following list may help you find applications that you have been missing*

1. *Faith:*

   What does the Bible passage teach me about personal faith?

   What do I learn about God, Jesus Christ, the Holy Spirit and my relationship to them?

   What specific truths should I believe? Why should I believe them?

2. *Attitudes:*

   What do I learn about good or bad attitudes? What are the results of each kind?

   What should be my attitudes? How can I change negative ones?

   What do I learn about emotions? Is there help suggested for destructive emotions such as fears, worries, hates, resentments, jealousies?

---

* From *The Joy of Discovery* by Oletta Wald,
Copyright 1956 by Bible Banner Press. Used by permission.

3. *Actions:*

   What should be my actions? Are there errors to avoid?
   Are there any actions I need to change?

4. *Sins:*

   What sins are pointed out in my life? Are there some which I
   need to confess to God? To my fellowmen? Which do I need
   to forsake?

5. *Examples:*

   What examples are there to follow? Not to follow? Why?

6. *Challenges:*

   What are some admonitions which I should make my own?

   How can I follow these admonitions in a concrete way? In my
   relationships in my home? In school? In work? With others?
   With friends?

7. *Promises:*

   What promises can I claim for my own?

   Are there any conditions which I must fulfill to claim these
   promises?

   Are there any specific prayer promises to claim?

Why Applications Are Difficult

Have you noticed how hard it is sometimes to write out an
application? The devil is delighted when people neglect to apply
what they learn in their Bible study. Although they think they have
had a good study, he knows that it won't make any difference.
Have you ever wondered why people hesitate to apply the Word?
Here are seven reasons:

1. *The human heart resists change.* Are you ready to change in
any area? Are you willing to accept rebuke about things that you
think are all right? Proverbs 15:31,32 says, "He whose ear heeds
wholesome admonition will abide among the wise. He who ignores
instruction despises himself, but he who heeds admonition gains
understanding."

2. *There is a lack of understanding of the meaning of
application.* The opposite of knowledge is not ignorance, but
disobedience. Scripturally, to know is to do!

3. *There is pressure from society to conform to relative standards, not absolutes.* You may say, "I watch television less than my non-Christian neighbor." The question is, however, have you examined your television watching habits in light of Matthew 6:33, "But seek first His kingdom . . ." and Psalm 101:3, "I will not set before my eyes anything that is base."

4. *It is easy to substitute interpretation for application.* This is especially true in the area of prophecy. There is profit in studying prophecy, but understanding and interpretation of all of the symbols is secondary to having your life purified. "And every one who thus hopes on Him purifies himself as He is pure" (I John 3:3).

5. *There is a tendency to apply the Word in areas where it is already being applied.* This is especially true when the sin mentioned is so general and universal that no specifics are used. For example, everyone could write an application concerning the area of pride every week. There isn't much meat to this type of application. A better application would be going to a friend to correct a story which you exaggerated due to pride.

6. *There is a tendency to substitute emotional experience for volitional action.* People talk about spiritual highs and spiritual lows. They usually mean emotional highs and emotional lows. It is possible to be emotionally low and spiritually high.

7. *There is a tendency to accept a human viewpoint rather than a divine viewpoint.* Psychiatrists, psychologists, sociologists, professors, doctors and a horde of other "experts" are attempting to define what normal behavior is. All of their counsel must be examined in the light of the Word. Christians are called to be holy even as Christ is holy, not to be normal even as everyone else is normal!

Extended Applications

As you grow in the Lord, it becomes increasingly important to apply the Word of God to your life. At the same time, it also becomes more difficult to become specific in your applications. At this point, you should be aware of the concept of spending weeks or even months on a single application.

It usually takes more than a week to deal with root attitudes. When the Holy Spirit has used the Word to reveal an attitude need, you will want to take plenty of time to adequately deal with yourself. For instance, self acceptance or sensitivity to others is not accomplished in one week.

The basic method of this type of application is not different from any other. You find out what the Bible says, how it applies to your life and what actions you are going to take. Here are some additional steps.

1. Break down your problem into its component parts. You may have to deal with these parts concurrently, but this will help you evaluate your progress.

2. Pray for insights into related areas of your life that need to be dealt with. Ask God to use people to expose several symptoms of the one problem you are working on.

3. Do extra Bible study on this subject or related subjects. Often a topical Bible study is very helpful at this point.

4. Read related books. Good books often can give practical suggestions and needed encouragement. However, be careful in your selection of books. Use books which are Christ-centered and based upon the Bible. Ask men of God whom you respect to help you make your selections.

5. Work on developing new habits. Root problems often have symptoms that are revealed in poor habits. Work on developing new ones.

6. Use others for checkup. If you are going to take several weeks on a single application, you will know you have made significant progress when someone who doesn't know about your application program remarks about the change that has occurred in your life. This is the greatest checkup and a true test of application.

WELL...
WHAT WOULD A
GOOD APPLICATION BE?

Summary:
Unit Three

Passage Description Methods
1. Vertical Chart
2. Personal Paraphrase
3. Detailed Outline
4. Creative Approaches

Observation Methods
1. Have the Right Mental Attitude
2. Consider Comparisons and Contrasts
3. Be Sensitive to Form and Structure
4. Notice Proportions
5. Record Repetitions
6. Visualize the Verbs
7. Picture the Illustrations
8. Examine the Explanations
9. Change Your Viewpoint

Verse-by-verse Meditation Methods
1. Defining Important Words
2. Questions and Answers
3. Cross-references

Theme and Conclusions Methods
1. How to Make a Thought Chain
2. How to Use a Topical Grid
3. How to Organize Your Study

Application Methods
1. Possible Areas of Application
2. Why Applications are Difficult
3. Extended Applications

STS BLANKS

Search the Scriptures blanks
may be purchased in quantities
of 25, 50 and 100 from:
Customer Services
NavPress
P.O. Box 1659
Colorado Springs, Colorado 80901

**FREE NAVIGATOR
DISCIPLESHIP MATERIALS CATALOG**

A catalog containing a listing
of other materials produced
by NavPress may also
be obtained by writing
the Customer Services Department.